Sorry You Have Crazy Friends!

and I'm One of Them

Copyright © 2026 G'Bryella Whyt

ISBN: [978-1-971419-22-0]

All rights reserved. No part of this publication may be reproduced, distributed, or transmitted in any form or by any means, including photocopying, recording, or other electronic or mechanical methods, without the prior written permission of the author, except in the case of brief quotations embodied in critical reviews and certain other noncommercial uses permitted by copyright law. For permission requests, write to the publisher at the address below: awestwood33@gmail.com This is a work of fiction. Names, characters, places, and incidents either are the product of the author's imagination or are used fictitiously. Any resemblance to actual persons, living or dead, events, or locales is entirely coincidental. Printed in [United States] Second Edition

Late Friend

"Sorry your friend is always late,
Not caring about your time, making you wait.

She thinks her time is more important than yours,
While you're waiting at the café, she's still doing chores.

So you sit and you stew, your coffee long cold,
While she's busy 'getting ready'—or so you've been told."

Drama Queen Friend

"Sorry your friend's a certified wreck,
Crying because BarBucks spelled her name as 'Beck.'

She's bawling in the corner over a text,
Convincing herself her life is hexed.

You'd run for the hills, but she'd call you a traitor,
So here you are—her unpaid crisis navigator."

Boring Friend

"Sorry your friend is boring as dirt,
Their idea of fun is ironing a shirt.

They'll tell you about tax deductions they've claimed,
And how Trader Joe's apples are insanely famed.

You'd rather get a colonoscopy on repeat,
Than hear about their fiber-packed Whole Wheat."

Flakey Friend

"Sorry your friend's the queen of no-shows,
She cancels for 'self-care'—what? Painting her toes?

Your car flipped over; you called her to cry,
She said, 'I'd help, but my hair's not dry.'

She blows up your phone when she's in despair,
But for your big moments? She's never there.

Excuses pile up like leaves on a tree,
But you stay—hell, you've known her since three."

Drunk Friend

"Sorry your friend's always drunk before nine,
Drinks whiskey like water, thinks everything's fine.

She's twerking on tables, flashing the band,
Then falling face-first into someone's nacho stand.

You're dragging her out while she slurs, 'Let's go!'
Still holding her drink and her busted stiletto."

Stoned Friend

"Sorry your friend's both stoned and divine,
Talking chakras and edibles at the same time.

She's spiritual, chill, and high as a kite,
While you're stressed out just trying to sleep at night.

You think she's wasting her life without a clue,
But damn it, she's still happier than you."

Annoying Rich Friend

"Sorry your friend is annoyingly rich,
Bragging about everything like a little bitch.

She flaunts her new yacht, her trip to Milan,
While you're just proud of your Groupon coupon.

You'd cut her loose, but you'd miss the free wine,
So you tolerate her—one glass at a time."

Gossip Friend

"Sorry your friend's a gossiping pro,
She knows who's slept with who—and their cousin Joe.

She'll spill your secrets for a shot of tequila,
Then whisper, 'Wait till you hear about Sheila!'

You'd cut her loose, but here's the twist,
Without her, you'd miss your weekly scandal list."

Competitive Friend

"Sorry your friend's a competitive queen,
Outdoing you with every damn thing you've seen.

You bought a car? They bought a plane.
You got a dog? They adopted a lion in Maine.

You got a promotion? They cured a disease,
And somehow made it about their degrees."

Negative Nancy Friend

"Sorry your friend's a tornado of dread,
Complains so much, you wish you were dead.

You say, 'Life's great!' They scowl, 'It's trash,'
And follow it up with a comment that's brash.

A black hole of doom, sucking air from the room,
Turning every good day into instant gloom."

Sad Friend

"She cries so much, it's a public spectacle,
She needs pills by the pound and a therapy schedule.

She doesn't look pretty when she starts to bawl,
Mascara rivers running down like a waterfall.

It's so embarrassing, I don't know what to do,
And now I wonder… does she cry during sex too?"

Copycat Friend

"Sorry your friend's your personal clone,
Stealing your style like a dog on a bone.

You bought a red bag? She bought it too,
You cut your hair? She's copying you!

She drives your car, she flirts with your guy,
She's Single White Female but amplified.

The Know-It-All Friend

"Sorry your friend's the queen of advice,
She'll tell you your cough needs 'garlic and ice.'

She's divorced three times but insists she's the pro,
Saying, 'Here's how to keep him,' as if she'd know.

Her kid's a menace, banned from four schools,
But she's lecturing you on having 'parenting rules.'"

The Funny Friend

"Your friend's a funny, chaotic mess,
But she's the one you truly love best.

She laughs at everything, brings the good vibes,
And always knows how to take your side.

You know under the jokes there's some pain,
But she'd be there for you—snow, sleet, or rain."

The Slut Friend

"Sorry your friend's always on Tinder,
She's swiping right like a serial sinner.

She sleeps with a guy at least twice a week,
And her body count's higher than a mountain peak.

She asks to sip your drink, but you back away,
'Cause swapping spit might lead to an STD buffet."

Ride or Die Friend

"She's your ride-or-die, through thick and thin,
Pulled you from heartbreaks and bottles of gin.

She's the one who bailed you out at 3 a.m.,
And told your ex, 'You'll never deserve her again!'

From jobs that sucked to nights that were rough,
She's proof that one friend is always enough."

"Your friends are disasters; let's not be coy,
Flakey, dramatic, and slutty—oh boy!

The stoned one's lost, the mooch has no cash,
The drunk's passed out in her sequined sash.

But without this crew of chaotic delight,
Your life would be lame every single night."

In a world that feels louder and more divided every day, here's to loving each other anyway.

Our friends don't always think like us, vote like us, or live like us — but we still need each other.
We're here to learn, grow, laugh, heal, and sometimes lose our minds together.

That's friendship. That's womanhood. That's life.
I love you all. Truly.

If this book made you smile, feel seen, or helped you in any small way, please consider leaving a review. It really helps another woman find this book when she might need it most.
Thank you for reading.
— G

www.ingramcontent.com/pod-product-compliance
Lightning Source LLC
LaVergne TN
LVHW070222080526
838202LV00068B/6885